Mediterranean Diet for Beginners

*Simple Healthy Recipes
for Eating Well Everyday*

TIFFANY WHEATLY

© **Copyright 2021 By Tiffany Wheatly - All rights reserved.**

The content contained within this book may not be reproduced, duplicated or transmitted without direct written permission from the author or the publisher. Under no circumstances will any blame or legal responsibility be held against the publisher, or author, for any damages, reparation, or monetary loss due to the information contained within this book. Either directly or indirectly.

Legal Notice:

This book is copyright protected. This book is only for personal use. You cannot amend, distribute, sell, use, quote or paraphrase any part, or the content within this book, without the consent of the author or publisher.

Disclaimer Notice:

Please note the information contained within this document is for educational and entertainment purposes only. All effort has been executed to present accurate, up to date, and reliable, complete information. No warranties of any kind are declared or implied. Readers acknowledge that the author is not engaging in the rendering of legal, financial, medical or professional advice. The content within this book has been derived from various sources. Please consult a licensed professional before attempting any techniques outlined in this book.

By reading this document, the reader agrees that under no circumstances is the author responsible for any losses, direct or indirect, which are incurred as a result of the use of information contained within this document, including, but not limited to, errors, omissions, or inaccuracies

Table Of Contents

INTRODUCTION 8

BREAKFAST RECIPES 12

    1. Western Omelette 13
    2. Scrambled Pancake Hash 15
    3. Morning Time Sausages 17
    4. Baked Bacon Egg Cups 19
    5. Breakfast Meatloaf Slices 21

LUNCH 24

    6. Shrimp and Lemon Sauce 25
    7. Shrimp and Beans Salad 27
    8. Pecan Salmon Fillets 29
    9. Salmon and Broccoli 31
    10. Salmon and Peach Pan 33

DINNER 35

    11. Moroccan Fish 36
    12. Nicoise-inspired Salad with Sardines 38
    13. Broiled Chili Calamari 40
    14. Salmon with Corn Pepper Salsa 42
    15. Seafood Paella 44

SIDE DISHES **48**

16. CABBAGE AND MUSHROOMS MIX 49
17. LEMON MUSHROOM RICE 50
18. PAPRIKA AND CHIVES POTATOES 52
19. BULGUR, KALE AND CHEESE MIX 54
20. SPICY GREEN BEANS MIX 56

VEGETABLES **59**

21. DELICIOUS TOMATO BROTH 60
22. RUSTIC CAULIFLOWER AND CARROT HASH 62
23. MOUSSAKA 64
24. VEGETABLE-STUFFED GRAPE LEAVES 66
25. GRILLED EGGPLANT ROLLS 69

APPETIZERS AND SNACKS **72**

26. MASCARPONE PECANS STUFFED DATES 73
27. PEPPERY POTATOES 76
28. CHEESY CAPRESE SALAD SKEWERS 78
29. LEAFY LACINATO TUSCAN TREAT 80
30. BURRATA CAPRESE STACK 81

DRINKS **84**

31. MANGO-PEAR SMOOTHIE 85
32. AVOCADO-BLUEBERRY SMOOTHIE 86
33. CRANBERRY-PUMPKIN SMOOTHIE 88

| 34. | Sweet Cranberry Nectar | 90 |
| 35. | Hearty Pear and Mango Smoothie | 92 |

DESSERTS 93

36.	Minty Coconut Cream	94
37.	Watermelon Cream	95
38.	Pistachio Balls	97
39.	Almonds and Oats Pudding	98
40.	Chocolate Cups	99

Introduction

You may be wondering what the Mediterranean diet is, and you should know that we consider it more of a lifestyle than a regular diet. It's a way of eating that will help you live a happy and full life. You can lose weight and strengthen your heart while providing yourself with all the nutrients you need for a long and healthy life. Those who follow this diet are often at lower risk for cancer, Alzheimer's, enjoy a longer lifespan and overall better cardiovascular health. The Mediterranean diet contains foods rich in healthy oils, full of vegetables and fruits, and foods low in saturated fat. It is a heart-healthy eating plan based on the food that can be found in the Mediterranean, which includes a good number of countries. It includes pasta, rice, vegetables and fruits, but does not allow much red meat. Nuts are also part of this diet, but they should be limited due to the fact that they are high in fat and calories. The Mediterranean diet limits fat consumption and discourages the consumption of saturated or trans fats. Both types have been linked to heart disease.

Some of the benefits include:

- **Memory Preservation** - Dementia and Alzheimer's disease cast their dark shadow over seniors living in all corners of the world. The sad thing is that once the disease sets in, there is no cure. Surprisingly, people in Mediterranean areas have managed to keep these ailments at bay. Even at the age of 95, seniors can recall their childhood memories. Because the Mediterranean diet is full of fresh ingredients, it prevents the brain from falling prey to these diseases.

- **Reduces cognitive decline** - As we age, brain cells are also prone to damage. It not only paves the way for memory problems, but also has other mental and physical symptoms. The healing properties of fresh ingredients, used in the preparation of Mediterranean foods, prevent damage and premature degeneration of brain cells. In addition to preventing memory loss, this diet will ensure you have overall healthy brain functions. The diet will also ensure increased production of brain cells. Thus, there will be a holistic development of your mental efficiency.

- **Prevention of heart problems** - Cardiovascular diseases are rampant among the adult population in the United States. Medical surveys show that a whopping 40% of all adults have some form of heart problem. These can be attributed to junk and processed food consumption. However, these numbers are lower in Mediterranean nations.

Again, their diet plays an important role in keeping their hearts active and disease-free. Selecting unprocessed ingredients, good, natural fats and a steady dose of wine keep the heart in perfect condition. The strong walls of the heart can pump oxygenated blood to all parts of the body, thus preventing any disease related to circulation. Continuously following the Mediterranean diet will help patients get rid of bad cholesterol. When LDL decreases, their heart functions will become better due to the lack of fatty deposits on the arteries.

- **Strong Bones** - It is common for people to lose the strength and texture of their bones as they age. While the percentage of patients who come in with bone fragility issues in the United States is high, the same is not true for people who follow Mediterranean eating patterns. Green leafy vegetables are a good source of calcium

Breakfast Recipes

1. Western Omelette

Preparation Time: 5 minutes

Cooking Time: 10 minutes

Servings: 4

Ingredients:

- 1 green pepper
- 5 eggs
- ½ yellow onion, diced
- 3-ounces Parmesan cheese, shredded
- 1 teaspoon butter
- 1 teaspoon oregano, dried
- 1 teaspoon cilantro, dried
- 1 teaspoon olive oil
- 3 tablespoons cream cheese

Directions:

1. In a bowl, add the eggs and whisk them. Sprinkle the cilantro, oregano, and cream cheese into the eggs.
2. Add the shredded parmesan and mix the egg mixture well.
3. Preheat your air fryer to 360°Fahrenheit. Pour the egg mixture into the air fryer basket tray and place it into the air fryer.
4. Cook the omelet for 10-minutes. Meanwhile, chop the green pepper and dice the onion. Pour olive oil into a skillet and preheat well over medium heat.
5. Add the chopped green pepper and onion to skillet and roast for 8-minutes. Stir veggies often.
6. Remove the omelet from air fryer basket tray and place it on a serving plate. Add the roasted vegetables and serve warm.

Nutrition: Calories: 204, Total Fat: 14.9g, Carbs: 4.3g, Protein: 14.8g

2. Scrambled Pancake Hash

Preparation Time: 1hour 15 minutes

Cooking Time: 9 minutes

Servings: 7

Ingredients:

- 1 egg
- ¼ cup heavy cream
- 5 tablespoons butter
- 1 cup coconut flour
- 1 teaspoon ground ginger
- 1 teaspoon salt
- 1 tablespoon apple cider vinegar
- 1 teaspoon baking soda

Directions:

1. Combine the salt, baking soda, ground ginger and flour in a mixing bowl. In a separate bowl crack, the egg into it. Add butter and heavy cream.
2. Mix well using a hand mixer. Combine the liquid and dry mixtures and stir until smooth. Preheat your air fryer to 400°Fahrenheit.
3. Pour the pancake mixture into the air fryer basket tray. Cook the pancake hash for 4-minutes.
4. After this, scramble the pancake hash well and continue to cook for another 5-minutes more. When dish is cooked, transfer it to serving plates, and serve hot!

Nutrition: Calories: 178, Total Fat: 13.3g, Carbs: 10.7g, Protein: 4.4g

3. Morning Time Sausages

Preparation Time: 15 minutes

Cooking Time: 12 minutes

Servings: 6

Ingredients:

- 7-ounces ground chicken
- 7-ounces ground pork
- 1 teaspoon ground coriander
- 1 teaspoon basil, dried
- ½ teaspoon nutmeg
- 1 teaspoon olive oil
- 1 teaspoon minced garlic
- 1 tablespoon coconut flour
- 1 egg

- 1 teaspoon soy sauce
- 1 teaspoon sea salt
- ½ teaspoon ground black pepper

Directions:

1. Combine the ground pork, chicken, soy sauce, ground black pepper, garlic, basil, coriander, nutmeg, sea salt, and egg.
2. Add the coconut flour and mix the mixture well to combine.
3. Preheat your air fryer to 360°Fahrenheit. Make medium-sized sausages with the ground meat mixture.
4. Spray the inside of the air fryer basket tray with the olive oil.
5. Place prepared sausages into the air fryer basket and place inside of air fryer. Cook the sausages for 6-minutes.
6. Turn the sausages over and cook for 6-minutes more.
7. When the cook time is completed, let the sausages chill for a little bit. Serve warm.

Nutrition: Calories: 156, Total Fat: 7.5g, Carbs: 1.3g, Protein: 20.2g

4. Baked Bacon Egg Cups

Preparation Time: 10 minutes

Cooking Time: 12 minutes

Servings: 2

Ingredients:

- 2 eggs
- 1 tablespoon chives, fresh, chopped
- ½ teaspoon paprika
- ½ teaspoon cayenne pepper
- 3-ounces cheddar cheese, shredded
- ½ teaspoon butter
- ¼ teaspoon salt
- 4-ounces bacon, cut into tiny pieces

Directions:

1. Slice bacon into tiny pieces and sprinkle it with cayenne pepper, salt, and paprika. Mix the chopped bacon.
2. Spread butter in bottom of ramekin dishes and beat the eggs there.
3. Add the chives and shredded cheese. Add the chopped bacon over egg mixture in ramekin dishes. Place the ramekins in your air fryer basket.
4. Preheat your air fryer to 360°Fahrenheit. Place the air fryer basket in your air fryer and cook for 12-minutes.
5. When the cook time is completed, remove the ramekins from air fryer and serve warm.

Nutrition: Calories: 553, Total Fat: 43.3g, Carbs: 2.3g, Protein: 37.3g

5. Breakfast Meatloaf Slices

Preparation Time: 10 minutes

Cooking Time: 20 minutes

Servings: 6

Ingredients:

- 8-ounces ground pork
- 7-ounces ground beef
- 1 teaspoon olive oil
- 1 teaspoon butter
- 1 tablespoon oregano, dried
- 1 teaspoon cayenne pepper
- 1 teaspoon salt
- 1 tablespoon chives

- 1 tablespoon almond flour
- 1 egg
- 1 onion, diced

Directions:

1. Beat egg in a bowl. Add the ground beef and ground pork.
2. Add the chives, almond flour, cayenne pepper, salt, dried oregano, and butter. Add diced onion to ground beef mixture.
3. Use hands to shape a meatloaf mixture. Preheat the air fryer to 350°Fahrenheit. Spray the inside of the air fryer basket with olive oil and place the meatloaf inside it.
4. Cook the meatloaf for 20-minutes. When the meatloaf has cooked, allow it to chill for a bit. Slice and serve it.

Nutrition: Calories: 176, Total Fat: 6.2g, Carbs: 3.4g, Protein: 22.2g

Lunch

6. Shrimp and Lemon Sauce

Preparation Time: 10 minutes

Cooking Time: 15 minutes

Servings: 4

Ingredients:

- 1-pound shrimp, peeled and deveined
- 1/3 cup lemon juice
- 4 egg yolks
- 2 tablespoons olive oil
- 1 cup chicken stock
- Salt and black pepper to the taste
- 1 cup black olives, pitted and halved
- 1 tablespoon thyme, chopped

Directions:

1. In a bowl, mix the lemon juice with the egg yolks and whisk well.
2. Heat up a pan with the oil over medium heat, add the shrimp and cook for 2 minutes on each side and transfer to a plate.
3. Heat up a pan with the stock over medium heat, add some of this over the egg yolks and lemon juice mix and whisk well.
4. Add this over the rest of the stock, also add salt and pepper, whisk well and simmer for 2 minutes.
5. Add the shrimp and the rest of the ingredients, toss and serve right away.

Nutrition: calories 237, fat 15.3, fiber 4.6, carbs 15.4, protein 7.6

7. Shrimp and Beans Salad

Preparation Time: 10 minutes

Cooking Time: 4 minutes

Servings: 4

Ingredients:

- 1-pound shrimp, peeled and deveined
- 30 ounces canned cannellini beans, drained and rinsed
- 2 tablespoons olive oil
- 1 cup cherry tomatoes, halved
- 1 teaspoon lemon zest, grated
- ½ cup red onion, chopped
- A pinch of salt and black pepper

For the dressing:

- 3 tablespoons red wine vinegar
- 2 garlic cloves, minced

- ½ cup olive oil

Directions:

1. Heat up a pan with 2 tablespoons oil over medium-high heat, add the shrimp and cook for 2 minutes on each side.
2. In a salad bowl, combine the shrimp with the beans and the rest of the ingredients except the ones for the dressing and toss.
3. In a separate bowl, combine the vinegar with ½ cup oil and the garlic and whisk well.
4. Pour over the salad, toss and serve right away.

Nutrition: calories 207, fat 12.3, fiber 6.6, carbs 15.4, protein 8.7

8. Pecan Salmon Fillets

Preparation Time: 10 minutes

Cooking Time: 15 minutes

Servings: 6

Ingredients:

- 3 tablespoons olive oil
- 3 tablespoons mustard
- 5 teaspoons honey
- 1 cup pecans, chopped
- 6 salmon fillets, boneless
- 1 tablespoon lemon juice
- 3 teaspoons parsley, chopped
- Salt and pepper to the taste

Directions:

1. In a bowl, mix the oil with the mustard and honey and whisk well.
2. Put the pecans and the parsley in another bowl.
3. Season the salmon fillets with salt and pepper, arrange them on a baking sheet lined with parchment paper, brush with the honey and mustard mix and top with the pecans mix.
4. Introduce in the oven at 400 degrees F, bake for 15 minutes, divide between plates, drizzle the lemon juice on top and serve.

Nutrition: calories 282, fat 15.5, fiber 8.5, carbs 20.9, protein 16.8

9. Salmon and Broccoli

Preparation Time: 10 minutes

Cooking Time: 20 minutes

Servings: 4

Ingredients:

- 2 tablespoons balsamic vinegar
- 1 broccoli head, florets separated
- 4 pieces salmon fillets, skinless
- 1 big red onion, roughly chopped
- 1 tablespoon olive oil
- Sea salt and black pepper to the taste

Directions:

1. In a baking dish, combine the salmon with the broccoli and the rest of the ingredients, introduce in the oven and bake at 390 degrees F for 20 minutes.

2. Divide the mix between plates and serve.

Nutrition: calories 302, fat 15.5, fiber 8.5, carbs 18.9, protein 19.8

10. Salmon and Peach Pan

Preparation Time: 10 minutes

Cooking Time: 11 minutes

Servings: 4

Ingredients:

- 1 tablespoon balsamic vinegar
- 1 teaspoon thyme, chopped
- 1 tablespoon ginger, grated
- 2 tablespoons olive oil
- Sea salt and black pepper to the taste
- 3 peaches, cut into medium wedges
- 4 salmon fillets, boneless

Directions:

1. Heat up a pan with the oil over medium-high heat, add the salmon and cook for 3 minutes on each side.
2. Add the vinegar, the peaches and the rest of the ingredients, cook for 5 minutes more, divide everything between plates and serve.

Nutrition: calories 293, fat 17.1, fiber 4.1, carbs 26.4, protein 24.5

Dinner

11. Moroccan Fish

Preparation Time: 9 minutes

Cooking Time: 76 minutes

Servings: 12

Ingredients:

- Garbanzo beans (15 oz. Can)
- Red bell peppers (2)
- Large carrot (1)
- Vegetable oil (1 tbsp.)
- Onion (1)
- Garlic (1 clove)
- Tomatoes (3 chopped/14.5 oz can)
- Olives (4 chopped)
- Chopped fresh parsley (.25 cup)
- Ground cumin (.25 cup)
- Paprika (3 tbsp.)
- Chicken bouillon granules (2 tbsp.)
- Cayenne pepper (1 tsp.)

- Salt (to your liking)
- Tilapia fillets (5 lb.)

Directions:

1. Drain and rinse the beans. Thinly slice the carrot and onion. Mince the garlic and chop the olives. Throw away the seeds from the peppers and cut them into strips.
2. Warm the oil in a frying pan using the medium temperature setting. Toss in the onion and garlic. Simmer them for approximately five minutes.
3. Fold in the bell peppers, beans, tomatoes, carrots, and olives.
4. Continue sautéing them for about five additional minutes.
5. Sprinkle the veggies with the cumin, parsley, salt, chicken bouillon, paprika, and cayenne.
6. Stir thoroughly and place the fish on top of the veggies.
7. Pour in water to cover the veggies.
8. Lower the heat setting and cover the pan to slowly cook until the fish is flaky (about 40 min.

Nutrition: Calories: 268 Protein: 42g Fat: 5g

12. Nicoise-inspired Salad with Sardines

Preparation Time: 9 minutes

Cooking Time: 16 minutes

Servings: 4

Ingredients:

- 4 eggs
- 12 ounces baby red potatoes (about 12 potatoes)
- 6 ounces green beans, halved
- 4 cups baby spinach leaves or mixed greens
- 1 bunch radishes, quartered (about 1 1/3 cups)
- 1 cup cherry tomatoes
- 20 Kalamata or Nicoise olives (about 1/3 cup)
- 3 (3.75-ounce) cans skinless, boneless sardines packed in olive oil, drained
- 8 tablespoons Dijon Red Wine Vinaigrette

Directions:

1. Situate the eggs in a saucepan and cover with water. Bring the water to a boil. Once the water starts to boil, close then turn the heat off. Set a timer for minutes.
2. Once the timer goes off, strain the hot water and run cold water over the eggs to cool. Peel the eggs when cool and cut in half.
3. Poke each potato a few times using fork. Place them on a microwave-safe plate and microwave on high for 4 to 5 minutes, until the potatoes are tender. Let cool and cut in half.
4. Place green beans on a microwave-safe plate and microwave on high for 1½ to 2 minutes, until the beans are crisp-tender. Cool.
5. Place 1 egg, ½ cup of green beans, 6 potato halves, 1 cup of spinach, 1/3 cup of radishes, ¼ cup of tomatoes, olives, and 3 sardines in each of 4 containers. Pour 2 tablespoons of vinaigrette into each of 4 sauce containers.

Nutrition: Calories: 450 Fat: 32g Protein: 21g

13. Broiled Chili Calamari

Preparation Time: 9 minutes

Cooking Time: 8 minutes

Servings: 4

Ingredients:

- 2 tablespoons extra virgin olive oil
- 1 teaspoon chili powder
- ½ teaspoon ground cumin
- Zest of 1 lime
- Juice of 1 lime
- Dash of sea salt
- 1 and ½ pounds squid, cleaned and split open, with tentacles cut into ½ inch rounds
- 2 tablespoons cilantro, chopped
- 2 tablespoons red bell pepper, minced

Directions:

1. Take a medium bowl and stir in olive oil, chili powder, cumin, lime zest, sea salt, lime juice and pepper

2. Add squid and let it marinade and stir to coat, coat and let it refrigerate for 1 hour
3. Pre-heat your oven to broil
4. Arrange squid on a baking sheet, broil for 8 minutes turn once until tender
5. Garnish the broiled calamari with cilantro and red bell pepper
6. Serve and enjoy!

Nutrition: Calories: 159 Fat: 13g Protein: 3g

14. Salmon with Corn Pepper Salsa

Preparation Time: 9 minutes

Cooking Time: 12 minutes

Servings: 2

Ingredients:

- 1 garlic clove, grated
- 1/2 teaspoon mild chili powder
- 1/2 teaspoon ground coriander
- 1.4 teaspoon ground cumin
- 2 limes – 1, zest and juice; 1 cut into wedges
- 2 teaspoons rapeseed oil
- 2 wild salmon fillets
- 1 ear of corn on the cob
- 1 red onion, finely chopped
- 1 avocado, cored, peeled, and finely chopped

- 1 red pepper, deseeded and finely chopped
- 1 red chili, halved and deseeded
- 1/2 a pack of finely chopped coriander

Directions:

1. Boil the corn in water for about 6-8 minutes until tender.
2. Drain and cut off the kernels.
3. In a bowl, combine garlic, spices, 1 tablespoon of lime juice, and oil; mix well to prepare spice rub.
4. Coat the salmon with the rub.
5. Add the zest to the corn and give it a gentle stir.
6. Heat a frying pan over medium heat.
7. Cook salmon for 4 minutes on both sides.
8. Serve the cooked salmon with salsa and lime wedges.
9. Enjoy!

Nutrition: Calories: 949 Fat: 57.4g Protein: 76.8g

15. Seafood Paella

Preparation Time: 9 minutes

Cooking Time: 41 minutes

Servings: 4

Ingredients:

- 4 small lobster tails (6-12 oz. each)
- 3 tbsp. Extra Virgin Olive Oil
- 1 large yellow onion
- 2 cups Spanish rice
- 4 garlic cloves
- 2 large pinches of Spanish saffron threads
- 1 tsp. Sweet Spanish paprika
- 1 tsp. cayenne pepper
- 1/2 tsp. Aleppo pepper flakes
- 2 large Roma tomatoes

- 6 oz. French green beans
- 1 lb. prawns or large shrimp
- 1/4 cup chopped fresh parsley

Directions:

1. Using big pot, add 3 cups of water and bring it to a rolling boil
2. Add in the lobster tails and allow boil briefly, about 1-minutes or until pink, remove from heat
3. Using tongs situate the lobster tails to a plate and Do not discard the lobster cooking water
4. Allow the lobster is cool, then remove the shell and cut into large chunks.
5. Using a deep pan or skillet over medium-high heat, add 3 tbsp olive oil
6. Add the chopped onions, sauté the onions for 2 minutes and then add the rice, and cook for 3 more minutes, stirring regularly
7. Then add in the lobster cooking water and the chopped garlic and, stir in the saffron and its soaking liquid, cayenne pepper, Aleppo pepper, paprika, and salt

8. Gently stir in the chopped tomatoes and green beans, bring to a boil and allow it to slightly reduce, then cover and cook over low heat for 20 minutes
9. Once done, uncover and spread the shrimp over the rice, push it into the rice slightly, add in a little water, if needed
10. Close and cook for 18 minutes
11. Then add in the cooked lobster chunks
12. Once the lobster is warmed through, remove from heat allow the dish to cool completely
13. Distribute among the containers, store for 2 days
14. To Serve: Reheat in the microwave for 1-2 minutes or until heated through. Garnish with parsley and enjoy!

Nutrition: Calories: 536 Fat: 26g Protein: 50g

Side Dishes

16.   Cabbage and Mushrooms Mix

Preparation Time: 10 minutes

Cooking Time: 15 minutes

Servings: 2

Ingredients:

- 1 yellow onion, sliced
- 2 tablespoons olive oil
- 1 tablespoon balsamic vinegar
- ½ pound white mushrooms, sliced
- 1 green cabbage head, shredded
- 4 spring onions, chopped
- Salt and black pepper to the taste

Directions:

1. Heat up a pan with the oil over medium heat, add the yellow onion and the spring onions and cook for 5 minutes.
2. Add the rest of the ingredients, cook everything for 10 minutes, divide between plates and serve.

Nutrition: 199 calories 4.5g fat 2.4g fiber 5.6g carbs 2.2g protein

17. Lemon Mushroom Rice

Preparation Time: 10 minutes

Cooking Time: 30 minutes

Servings: 4

Ingredients:

- 2 cups chicken stock
- 1 yellow onion, chopped
- ½ pound white mushrooms, sliced
- 2 garlic cloves, minced
- 8 ounces wild rice
- Juice and zest of 1 lemon
- 1 tablespoon chives, chopped
- 6 tablespoons goat cheese, crumbled
- Salt and black pepper to the taste

Directions:

1. Heat up a pot with the stock over medium heat, add the rice, onion and the rest of the ingredients except the chives and the cheese, bring to a simmer and cook for 25 minutes. Add the remaining ingredients, cook everything for 5 minutes, divide between plates and serve as a side dish.

Nutrition: 222 calories 5.5g fat 5.4g fiber 12.3g carbs 5.6g protein

18. Paprika and Chives Potatoes

Preparation Time: 10 minutes

Cooking Time: 1 hour and 8 minutes

Servings: 4

Ingredients:

- 4 potatoes, scrubbed and pricked with a fork
- 1 tablespoon olive oil
- 1 celery stalk, chopped
- 2 tomatoes, chopped
- 1 teaspoon sweet paprika
- Salt and black pepper to the taste
- 2 tablespoons chives, chopped

Directions:

1. Arrange the potatoes on a baking sheet lined with parchment paper, introduce in the oven and bake at 350 degrees F for 1 hour. Cool the potatoes down, peel and cut them into larger cubes. Heat up a pan with the oil over medium heat, add the celery and the tomatoes and sauté for 2 minutes.

Add the potatoes and the rest of the ingredients, toss, cook everything for 6 minutes, divide the mix between plates and serve as a side dish.

Nutrition: 233 calories 8.7g fat 4.5g fiber 14.4g carbs 6.4g protein

19. Bulgur, Kale and Cheese Mix

Preparation Time: 10 minutes

Cooking Time: 10 minutes

Servings: 6

Ingredients:

- 4 ounces bulgur
- 4 ounces kale, chopped
- 1 tablespoon mint, chopped
- 3 spring onions, chopped
- 1 cucumber, chopped
- A pinch of allspice, ground
- 2 tablespoons olive oil
- Zest and juice of ½ lemon
- 4 ounces feta cheese, crumbled

Directions:

1. Put bulgur in a bowl, cover with hot water, aside for 10 minutes and fluff with a fork. Heat up a pan with the oil over medium heat, add the onions and the allspice and cook for 3 minutes.

2. Add the bulgur and the rest of the ingredients, cook everything for 5-6 minutes more, divide between plates and serve.

Nutrition: 200 calories 6.7g fat 3.4g fiber 15.4g carbs 4.5g protein

20. Spicy Green Beans Mix

Preparation Time: 5 minutes

Cooking Time: 15 minutes

Servings: 4

Ingredients:

- 4 teaspoons olive oil
- 1 garlic clove, minced
- ½ teaspoon hot paprika
- ¾ cup veggie stock
- 1 yellow onion, sliced
- 1-pound green beans, trimmed and halved
- ½ cup goat cheese, shredded
- 2 teaspoon balsamic vinegar

Directions:

1. Heat up a pan with the oil over medium heat, add the garlic, stir and cook for 1 minute. Add the green beans and the rest of the ingredients, toss, cook everything for 15 minutes more, divide between plates and serve as a side dish.

Nutrition: 188 calories 4g fat 3g fiber 12.4g carbs 4.4g protein

Vegetables

21.   Delicious Tomato Broth

Preparation Time: 10 minutes

Cooking Time: 15 minutes

Servings: 2

Ingredients:

- 14 oz can fire-roasted tomatoes
- ½ tsp dried basil
- ½ cup heavy cream
- ½ cup parmesan cheese, grated
- 1 cup cheddar cheese, grated
- 1 ½ cups vegetable stock
- ¼ cup zucchini, grated
- ½ tsp dried oregano
- Pepper
- Salt

Directions:

1. Add tomatoes, stock, zucchini, oregano, basil, pepper, and salt into the instant pot and stir well.
2. Seal pot and cook on high pressure for 5 minutes.
3. Release pressure using quick release. Remove lid.
4. Set pot on sauté mode. Add heavy cream, parmesan cheese, and cheddar cheese and stir well and cook until cheese is melted.
5. Serve and enjoy.

Nutrition: 460 Calories 35g Fat 24g Protein

22. Rustic Cauliflower and Carrot Hash

Preparation Time: 10 minutes

Cooking Time: 10 minutes

Servings: 4

Ingredients:

- 1 large onion, chopped
- 1 tablespoon garlic, minced
- 2 cups carrots, diced
- 4 cups cauliflower pieces, washed
- ½ teaspoon ground cumin

Directions:

1. Using big skillet over medium heat, cook 3 tbsps. of olive oil, onion, garlic, and carrots for 3 minutes.
2. Cut the cauliflower into 1-inch or bite-size pieces. Add the cauliflower, salt, and cumin to the skillet and toss to combine with the carrots and onions.
3. Cover and cook for 3 minutes.
4. Throw the vegetables and continue to cook uncovered for an additional 3 to 4 minutes.
5. Serve warm.

Nutrition: 159 Calories 3g Protein 15g Carbohydrates

23.   Moussaka

Preparation Time: 55 minutes

Cooking Time: 40 minutes

Servings: 6

Ingredients:

- 2 large eggplants, onions
- 10 cloves garlic, sliced
- 2 (15-ounce) cans diced tomatoes
- 1 (16-ounce) can garbanzo beans
- 1 teaspoon dried oregano

Directions:

1. Slice the eggplant horizontally into ¼-inch-thick round disks. Sprinkle the eggplant slices with 1 teaspoon of salt and place in a colander for 31minutes.

2. Preheat the oven to 450°F. Pat the slices of eggplant dry with a paper towel and spray each side with an olive oil spray or lightly brush each side with olive oil.
3. Spread eggplant in a layer on a baking sheet. Bake for 10 minutes.
4. With a spatula, turn it over and bake for 12 minutes.
5. Using big skillet add the olive oil, onions, garlic, and remaining 1 teaspoon of salt. Cook for 3 minutes. Add the tomatoes, garbanzo beans, oregano, and black pepper. Simmer for 11 minutes.
6. Using a deep casserole dish, begin to layer, starting with eggplant, then the sauce. Repeat until all ingredients have been used. Bake in the oven for 20 minutes.
7. Remove from the oven and serve warm.

Nutrition: 262 Calories 8g Protein 35g Carbohydrates

24. Vegetable-Stuffed Grape Leaves

Preparation Time: 50 minutes

Cooking Time: 45 minutes

Servings: 7

Ingredients:

- 2 cups white rice, rinsed
- 2 large tomatoes, finely diced
- 1 (16-ounce) jar grape leaves
- 1 cup lemon juice
- 4 to 6 cups water

Directions:

1. Incorporate rice, tomatoes, 1 onion, 1 green onion, 1 cup of parsley, 3 garlic cloves, salt, and black pepper.
2. Drain and rinse the grape leaves.
3. Prepare a large pot by placing a layer of grape leaves on the bottom. Lay each leaf flat and trim off any stems.
4. Place 2 tablespoons of the rice mixture at the base of each leaf. Fold over the sides, then roll as tight as possible. Situate the rolled grape leaves in the pot, lining up each rolled grape leaf. Continue to layer in the rolled grape leaves.
5. Gently pour the lemon juice and olive oil over the grape leaves, and add enough water to cover the grape leaves by 1 inch.
6. Lay a heavy plate that is smaller than the opening of the pot upside down over the grape leaves. Cover the pot and cook the leaves over medium-low heat for 45 minutes. Let stand for 20 minutes before serving.
7. Serve warm or cold.

Nutrition: 532 Calories 12g Protein 80g Carbohydrates

25. Grilled Eggplant Rolls

Preparation Time: 30 minutes

Cooking Time: 10 minutes

Servings: 5

Ingredients:

- 2 large eggplants
- 4 ounces goat cheese
- 1 cup ricotta
- ¼ cup fresh basil, finely chopped

Directions:

1. Slice the tops of the eggplants off and cut the eggplants lengthwise into ¼-inch-thick slices. Sprinkle the slices with the salt and place the eggplant in a colander for 15 to 20 minutes.
2. In a large bowl, combine the goat cheese, ricotta, basil, and pepper.
3. Preheat a grill, grill pan, or lightly oiled skillet on medium heat. Pat the eggplant slices dry using paper towel and lightly spray with olive oil spray.

Place the eggplant on the grill, grill pan or skillet and cook for 3 minutes on each side.
4. Take out the eggplant from the heat and let cool for 5 minutes.
5. To roll, lay one eggplant slice flat, place a tablespoon of the cheese mixture at the base of the slice, and roll up. Serve immediately or chill until serving.

Nutrition: 255 Calories 15g Protein 19g Carbohydrates

Appetizers and Snacks

26. Mascarpone Pecans Stuffed Dates

Preparation Time: 5 minutes

Cooking Time: 5 minutes

Servings: 12 to 15

Ingredients:

- 1 cup pecans, shells removed
- 1 (8-ounce) container Mascarpone cheese
- 20 medjool dates

Directions:

1. Preheat the oven to 350ºF (180ºC). Put the pecans on a baking sheet and bake for 5 to 6 minutes, until lightly toasted and aromatic. Take the pecans out of the oven and let cool for 5 minutes.

2. Once cooled, put the pecans in a food processor fitted with a chopping blade and chop until they resemble the texture of bulgur wheat or coarse sugar.
3. Reserve ¼ cup of ground pecans in a small bowl. Pour the remaining chopped pecans into a larger bowl and add the Mascarpone cheese.
4. Using a spatula, mix the cheese with the pecans until evenly combined.
5. Spoon the cheese mixture into a piping bag.
6. Using a knife, cut one side of the date lengthwise, from the stem to the bottom. Gently open and remove the pit.
7. Using the piping bag, squeeze a generous amount of the cheese mixture into the date where the pit used to be. Close up the date and repeat with the remaining dates.
8. Dip any exposed cheese from the stuffed dates into the reserved chopped pecans to cover it up.
9. Set the dates on a serving plate; serve immediately or chill in the fridge until you are ready to serve.

Nutrition: Calories: 253; Protein: 2g; Total Carbohydrates: 31g; Sugars: 27g; Fiber: 4g; Total Fat: 15g; Saturated Fat: 4g; Cholesterol: 27mg; Sodium: 7mg

27. Peppery Potatoes

Preparation Time: 10 minutes

Cooking Time: 18 minutes

Servings: 4

Ingredients:

- 4-pcs large potatoes, cubed
- 4-tbsp extra-virgin olive oil (divided)
- 3-tbsp garlic, minced
- ½-cup coriander or cilantro, finely chopped
- 2-tbsp fresh lemon juice
- 1¾-tbsp paprika
- 2-tbsp parsley, minced

Directions:

1. Place the potatoes in a microwave-safe dish. Pour over a tablespoon of olive oil. Cover the dish tightly with plastic wrap. Heat the potatoes for seven minutes in your microwave to par-cook them.
2. Cook 2 tablespoons of olive oil in a pan placed over medium-low heat. Add the garlic and cover. Cook for 3 minutes. Add the coriander, and cook 2 minutes.

Transfer the garlic-coriander sauce in a bowl, and set aside.

3. In the same pan placed over medium heat, heat 1 tablespoon of olive oil. Add the par-cooked potatoes. Do not stir! Cook for 3 minutes until browned, flipping once with a spatula. Continue cooking until browning all the sides.
4. Take out the potatoes and place them on a dish. Pour over the garlic-coriander sauce and lemon juice. Add the paprika, parsley, and salt. Toss gently to coat evenly.

<u>Nutrition</u>: 316.2 Calories 14.2g Fats 4.5g Protein

28.   Cheesy Caprese Salad Skewers

Preparation Time: 15 minutes

Cooking Time: 0 minute

Servings: 10

Ingredients:

- 8-oz cherry tomatoes, sliced in half
- A handful of fresh basil leaves, rinsed and drained
- 1-lb fresh mozzarella, cut into bite-sized slices
- Balsamic vinegar
- Extra virgin olive oil
- Freshly ground black pepper

Directions:

1. Sandwich a folded basil leaf and mozzarella cheese between the halves of tomato onto a toothpick.

2. Drizzle with olive oil and balsamic vinegar each skewer. To serve, sprinkle with freshly ground black pepper.

Nutrition: 94 Calories 3.7g Fats 2.1g Protein

29. Leafy Lacinato Tuscan Treat

Preparation Time: 10 minutes

Cooking Time: 0 minute

Servings: 1

Ingredients:

- 1-tsp Dijon mustard
- 1-tbsp light mayonnaise
- 3-pcs medium-sized Lacinato kale leaves
- 3-oz. cooked chicken breast, thinly sliced
- 6-bulbs red onion, thinly sliced
- 1-pc apple, cut into 9-slices

Directions:

1. Mix the mustard and mayonnaise until fully combined.
2. Spread the mixture generously on each of the kale leaves. Top each leaf with 1-oz. chicken slices, 3-apple slices, and 2-red onion slices. Roll each kale leaf into a wrap.

Nutrition: 370 Calories 14g Fats 29g Protein

30. Burrata Caprese Stack

Preparation Time: 5 minutes

Cooking Time: 0 minutes

Servings: 4

Ingredients:

- 1 large organic tomato
- ½ teaspoon salt
- ¼ teaspoon black pepper
- 1 (4-ounce) ball burrata cheese
- 8 fresh basil leaves
- 2 tablespoons extra-virgin olive oil
- 1 tablespoon red wine

Directions:

1. Slice the tomato into 4 thick slices, removing any tough center core and sprinkle with salt and pepper. Place the tomatoes, seasoned-side up, on a plate.
2. On a separate rimmed plate, slice the burrata into 4 thick slices and place one slice on top of each tomato slice.

Top each with one-quarter of the basil and pour any reserved burrata cream from the rimmed plate over top.
3. Drizzle with olive oil and vinegar and serve with a fork and knife.

Nutrition: 153 Calories 13g Fat 7g Protein 6g Carbohydrates

Drinks

31. Mango-Pear Smoothie

Preparation Time: 10 minutes

Cooking Time: 0 minutes

Servings: 1

Ingredients:

- 1 ripe pear, cored and chopped
- ½ mango, peeled, pitted, and chopped
- 1 cup chopped kale
- ½ cup plain Greek yogurt
- 2 ice cubes

Directions:

1. In a blender, purée the pear, mango, kale, and yogurt.
2. Add the ice and blend until thick and smooth. Pour the smoothie into a glass and serve cold.

Nutrition: Calories: 293; Total Fat: 8g; Saturated Fat: 5g; Carbohydrates: 53g; Fiber: 7g; Protein: 8g

32. Avocado-Blueberry Smoothie

Preparation Time: 5 minutes

Cooking Time: 0 minutes

Servings: 2

Ingredients:

- ½ cup unsweetened vanilla almond milk
- ½ cup low-fat plain Greek yogurt
- 1 ripe avocado, peeled, pitted, and coarsely chopped
- 1 cup blueberries
- ¼ cup gluten-free rolled oats
- ½ teaspoon vanilla extract
- 4 ice cubes

Directions:

1. In a blender, combine the almond milk, yogurt, avocado, blueberries, oats, and vanilla and pulse until well blended.
2. Add the ice cubes and blend until thick and smooth. Serve.

Nutrition: Calories: 273; Total fat: 15g; Saturated fat: 2g; Carbohydrates: 28g; Sugar: 10g; Fiber: 9g; Protein: 10g

33. Cranberry-Pumpkin Smoothie

Preparation Time: 5 minutes

Cooking Time: 0 minutes

Servings: 2

Ingredients:

- 2 cups unsweetened almond milk
- 1 cup pure pumpkin purée
- ¼ cup gluten-free rolled oats
- ¼ cup pure cranberry juice (no sugar added)
- 1 tablespoon honey
- ¼ teaspoon ground cinnamon
- Pinch ground nutmeg

Directions:

1. In a blender, combine the almond milk, pumpkin, oats, cranberry juice, honey, cinnamon, and nutmeg and blend until smooth.
2. Pour into glasses and serve immediately.

Nutrition: Calories: 190; Total fat: 7g; Saturated fat: 0g; Carbohydrates: 26g; Sugar: 12g; Fiber: 5g; Protein: 4g

34. Sweet Cranberry Nectar

Preparation Time: 8 minutes

Cooking Time: 5 minutes

Servings: 4

Ingredients:

- 4 cups fresh cranberries
- 1 fresh lemon juice
- ½ cup agave nectar
- 1 piece of cinnamon stick
- 1-gallon water, filtered

Directions:

1. Add cranberries, ½ gallon water, and cinnamon into your pot
2. Close the lid
3. Cook on HIGH pressure for 8 minutes
4. Release the pressure naturally

5. Firstly, strain the liquid, then add remaining water
6. Cool, add agave nectar and lemon
7. Served chill and enjoy!

Nutrition: Calories: 184 Fat: 0g Carbohydrates: 49g Protein: 1g

35.   Hearty Pear and Mango Smoothie

Preparation Time: 10 minutes

Cooking Time: 0

Servings: 1

Ingredients:

- 1 ripe mango, cored and chopped
- ½ mango, peeled, pitted and chopped
- 1 cup kale, chopped
- ½ cup plain Greek yogurt
- 2 ice cubes

Directions:

1. Add pear, mango, yogurt, kale, and mango to a blender and puree.
2. Add ice and blend until you have a smooth texture.
3. Serve and enjoy!

Nutrition: Calories: 293 Fat: 8g Carbohydrates: 53g Protein: 8g

Desserts

36. Minty Coconut Cream

Preparation Time: 4 minutes

Cooking Time: 0 minutes

Servings: 2

Ingredients:

- 1 banana, peeled
- 2 cups coconut flesh, shredded
- 3 tablespoons mint, chopped
- 1 and ½ cups coconut water
- 2 tablespoons stevia
- ½ avocado, pitted and peeled

Directions:

1. In a blender, combine the coconut with the banana and the rest of the ingredients, pulse well, divide into cups and serve cold.

Nutrition: Calories 193; Fat 5.4 g; Fiber 3.4 g; Carbs 7.6 g; Protein 3 g

37. Watermelon Cream

Preparation Time: 15 minutes

Cooking Time: 0 minutes

Servings: 2

Ingredients:

- 1-pound watermelon, peeled and chopped
- 1 teaspoon vanilla extract
- 1 cup heavy cream
- 1 teaspoon lime juice
- 2 tablespoons stevia

Directions:

1. In a blender, combine the watermelon with the cream and the rest of the ingredients, pulse well, divide into cups and keep in the fridge for 15 minutes before serving.

Nutrition: Calories 122; Fat 5.7 g; Fiber 3.2 g; Carbs 5.3 g; Protein 0.4 g

38. Pistachio Balls

Preparation Time: 10 minutes

Cooking Time: 5 minutes

Servings: 16

Ingredients:

- ½ cup pistachios, unsalted
- 1 cup dates, pitted
- ½ tsp ground fennel seeds
- ½ cup raisins
- Pinch of pepper

Directions:

1. Add all ingredients into the food processor and process until well combined.
2. Make small balls and place onto the baking tray.
3. Serve and enjoy.

Nutrition: Calories 55, Fat 0.9g, Carbohydrates 12.5g, Sugar 9.9g, Protein 0.8g, Cholesterol 0mg

39. Almonds and Oats Pudding

Preparation Time: 10 minutes

Cooking Time: 15 minutes

Servings: 4

Ingredients:

- 1 tablespoon lemon juice
- Zest of 1 lime
- 1 and ½ cups almond milk
- 1 teaspoon almond extract
- ½ cup oats
- 2 tablespoons stevia
- ½ cup silver almonds, chopped

Directions:

1. In a pan, combine the almond milk with the lime zest and the other ingredients, whisk, bring to a simmer and cook over medium heat for 15 minutes.
2. Divide the mix into bowls and serve cold.

Nutrition: Calories 174 Fat 12.1 Fiber 3.2 Carbs 3.9 Protein 4.8

40. Chocolate Cups

Preparation Time: 2 hours

Cooking Time: 0 minutes

Servings: 6

Ingredients:

- ½ cup avocado oil
- 1 cup, chocolate, melted
- 1 teaspoon matcha powder
- 3 tablespoons stevia

Directions:

1. In a bowl, mix the chocolate with the oil and the rest of the ingredients, whisk really well, divide into cups and keep in the freezer for 2 hours before serving.

Nutrition: Calories 174 Fat 9.1 Fiber 2.2 Carbs 3.9 Protein 2.8

www.ingramcontent.com/pod-product-compliance
Lightning Source LLC
Chambersburg PA
CBHW070940080526
44589CB00013B/1592